**PENGUIN CORE CONCEP**

Dear Educators, Parents, and Caregivers,

Welcome to Penguin Core Concepts! The Core Concepts program exposes children to a diverse range of literary and informational texts, which will help them develop important literacy and cognitive skills necessary to meet many of the Common Core State Standards (CCSS).

The Penguin Core Concepts program includes twenty concepts (shown on the inside front cover of this book), which cover major themes that are taught in the early grades. Each book in the program is assigned one or two core concepts, which tie into the content of that particular book.

Hard Hat Zone covers the concepts Community Workers & Helpers and Problem Solving. The social studies concept Community Workers & Helpers can be used as a way to expose students to a diverse range of literary and informational texts, as recommended in the CCSS for English Language Arts and Literacy. The concept Problem Solving can help students develop important cognitive skills necessary to meet many of the CCSS, such as how to apply problem-solving skills to decipher unfamiliar vocabulary. After you've read the book, here are some questions/ideas to get your discussion started:

- There are many different workers (humans and trucks) described in this book. Discuss their individual jobs, and how they work together to get the job done.

- This book has many vocabulary words which may be unfamiliar to the children. Using picture clues, context clues, and a dictionary, come up with definitions for the following words: *barricades, clods, counterweight, debris, haul, jointed, lopsided, rotating, rugged,* and *transporting*.

Above all, the books in the Penguin Core Concepts program have engaging stories with fantastic illustrations and/or photographs, and are a perfect way to instill the love of reading in a child!

Bonnie Bader, EdM
Editor in Chief, Penguin Core Concepts

HARD HAT ZONE

by Theo Baker

Grosset & Dunlap
An Imprint of Penguin Group (USA) LLC

This book is dedicated to the people who build things,
and, as always, my girls: Sarah and Anarres—TB

GROSSET & DUNLAP
Published by the Penguin Group
Penguin Group (USA) LLC, 375 Hudson Street, New York, New York 10014, USA

USA | Canada | UK | Ireland | Australia | New Zealand | India | South Africa | China

penguin.com
A Penguin Random House Company

Photo credits: cover, page 1: © Thinkstock, photo by Dragunov1981; cover, pages 1, 2, 4, 6–10, 13–15, 18–19, 22–26, 28–29: (brushed metal) © Thinkstock, photo by Andrey Kuzmin; back cover: (construction barrier) © Thinkstock, photo by eabff; back cover: (sign) © Thinkstock, photo by FootToo; page 3: © Thinkstock, photo by Hemera Technologies; page 4: © Thinkstock, photo by zefart; pages 5, 7, 9, 11, 13, 17, 26, 31: (cloud) © Thinkstock, art by Faruk SISKO; page 5: © Thinkstock, photo by thanapun watcharapanich; page 6: © Thinkstock, photo by pedrosala; page 7: © Thinkstock, photo by Laks-Art; page 8: © Thinkstock, photo by kynny; page 9: © Thinkstock, photo by Digital Vision; page 10: © Thinkstock, photo by Nirian; page 11: © Thinkstock, photo by Digital Vision; page 12: © Thinkstock, photo by ssgrafika; page 13: (bulldozers) © Thinkstock, photo by photochecker; page 13: (background) © Thinkstock, photo by Maksymowicz; page 14: © Thinkstock, photo by Palle Porila; page 15: © Thinkstock, photo by joel-t; pages 16–17: © Thinkstock, photo by progat; page 18: © Thinkstock, photo by Paul Vasarhelyi; page 19: © Thinkstock, photo by mrak_hr; pages 20–21: © Thinkstock, photo by potowizard; pages 22–23: © Thinkstock, photo by william87; page 24: © Thinkstock, photo by Vincent_St_Thomas; page 25: © Thinkstock, photo by Ingram Publishing; page 26: © Thinkstock, photo by photo by gece33; page 27: © Thinkstock, photo by Evgeniy Pavlenko; page 28: © Thinkstock, photo by thanapun; page 29: © Thinkstock, photo by Digital Vision; page 30: © Thinkstock, photo by TonyLomas; page 31: © Thinkstock, photo by Ingram Publishing; page 32: © Thinkstock, photo by Digital Vision.

Library of Congress Cataloging-in-Publication Data is available.

ISBN 978-0-448-47923-1 (pbk)   10 9 8 7 6 5 4 3 2 1
ISBN 978-0-448-47924-8 (hc)   10 9 8 7 6 5 4 3 2 1

Engines growl. Machines beep. Hammers strike concrete. On the other side of the fence, a construction crew is hard at work.

"Watch your step!"

"Clear a path!"

"Look alive down there!"

Want to see what's going on? Then step into the hard hat zone!

Look, a skyscraper is going up! When it's done, it will stretch over eight hundred feet into the sky. But the first job is to dig a deep hole for the foundation.

A simple hand shovel won't do.

Call in the excavator!

Foreman's Fact:
Don't ever, **ever** go into a construction site without adult supervision and the foreman's say-so. If a friendly foreman like me sees you without a hard hat, he won't have a friendly way to say, "Get off my site!"

The **excavator** is a heavy-duty digging machine. It has a long metal arm connected to a rotating platform. The rotating platform lets the operator swing around in any direction to dig with the jointed arm.

The operator drives the toothed bucket deep into the ground, lifts up the dirt, swings around, and unloads the dirt onto a giant pile.

Foreman's Fact: The giant pile where the bucket unloads the dirt is called the *dumping point*.

Here comes the front-end loader. It rolls and rumbles onto the site to clean up the huge dirt piles left by the excavator.

A **front-end loader** is a tractor with a wide square bucket mounted to the front. Besides cleaning up, its toothed bucket is great for transporting construction equipment, such as wood pallets, jackhammers, and generators, around the site.

Foreman's Fact: In our trade, we call construction trucks *heavy equipment*.

The front-end loader has dropped almost 65,000 pounds of earth into a **dump truck**.

It's time to haul out and take the debris to the city dump.

Before leaving the site, this eight-wheeled dump truck drives through a tire bath. This cleans the wheels of any dirt clods and rocks that could damage the roads.

Foreman's Fact:
A dump truck and its load must weigh less than 80,000 pounds to be allowed to travel outside the site without a special permit or license. Too much weight could damage roads and bridges.

At the dump, the driver tilts the rear bed of the truck, and the debris tumbles out in a cloud of dust. Then the driver heads back to the site for the next heavy load.

The excavator has dug down to the bedrock, a layer of solid rock beneath the ground. It's almost time to lay the foundation. But there's still one job left, and only one truck is rugged enough to do it: the bulldozer.

The **bulldozer** must turn all that bumpy, lopsided earth at the bottom of the hole into a flat and even surface. This is called *grading*.

The bulldozer's powerful blade scrapes along the ground, pushes away the rubble, and leaves a smooth surface in its tracks.

Foreman's Fact:
Back in the nineteenth century, a "bull dose" was a dose of medicine strong enough to knock out a bull. That's where the strange name of *bulldozer* comes from.

Now that the bulldozer has smoothed the ground, it's time to lay the foundation. A good foundation will help support the weight of the skyscraper and keep it sturdy.

The excavator crawls back in, but this time its bucket has been replaced with an auger drill. It uses this jumbo-size screw to drill several holes into the bedrock.

Dozens of long steel poles, called *piles*, are fitted into the holes. The foreman sends in the **pile driver**.

This machine pounds the poles deep into the bedrock. Using a pulley, it raises a weight high over the pole and sends the weight screaming downward. *ThhhhWACK!*

The foreman radios the concrete-mixer truck. It is across town at the ready-mix plant, getting its rear drum loaded with sand, gravel, and cement paste. Water is then added to the mixture, and the drum starts spinning. As the driver heads over to the site, the wet materials mix into concrete.

Foreman's Fact:
Want to know how concrete and cement are different? Concrete is a mixture of sand and gravel bound by a paste of water and cement. Cement is a binding agent made of limestone, calcium sulfate, and other trace minerals, which are heated in a kiln and then ground into a powder.

At the site, a long open tube called a *chute* extends from the rear of the truck to the bedrock. The driver sets the drum spinning the opposite direction. This reverse in motion forces the wet concrete out of the drum. The crew must hurry because in only a few minutes the concrete will start to harden inside the drum. If it does, they'll need dynamite to bust it out.

The wet concrete flows down the chute. The crew pours it over the bedrock and around the poles. The concrete starts hardening immediately, but it will take twenty-eight days for the concrete to become rock solid.

Once the concrete is rock solid, the foundation is finished.

Next, the underground pipes are laid.

Now it's time to start building up!

But how can we get up so high? By using cranes. **Cranes** help lift heavy construction materials to the upper levels.

The operator controls this truck-mounted crane from a cab. Special members of the crew called *riggers* help load metal beams onto the crane's hook. The beams will become the skeleton of the skyscraper.

When the load is secure, the crane lifts the beams, swings around, and hoists the load up to the helpers waiting on the second story.

The building is so tall now that the truck-mounted crane can't reach the upper levels. So why is the truck-mounted crane still working?

It is building its replacement: **the tower crane**!

With the help of the truck-mounted crane, special ironworkers are putting the tower crane together piece by piece.

The tower crane gets taller and taller. Once it passes about 265 feet in height, it will have to be joined to the building for support.

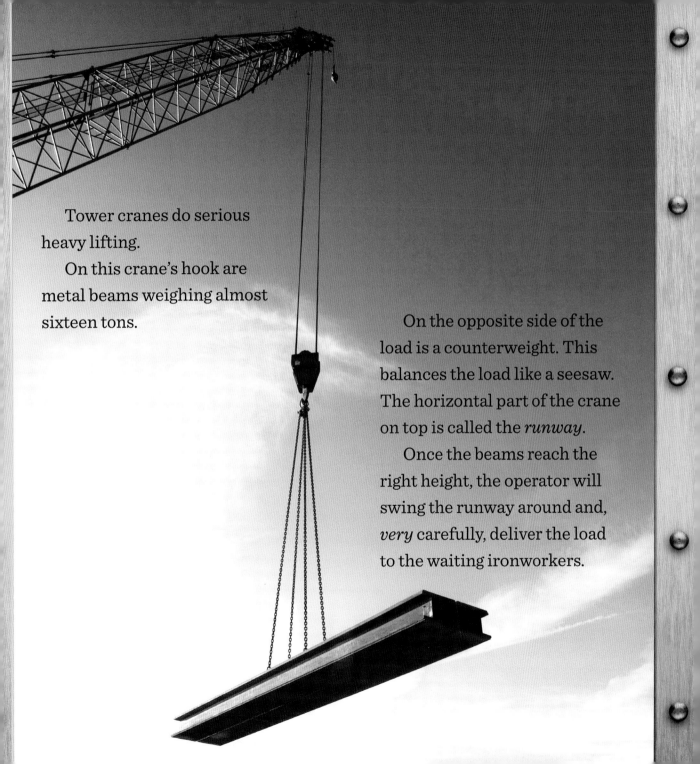

Tower cranes do serious heavy lifting.

On this crane's hook are metal beams weighing almost sixteen tons.

On the opposite side of the load is a counterweight. This balances the load like a seesaw. The horizontal part of the crane on top is called the *runway*.

Once the beams reach the right height, the operator will swing the runway around and, *very* carefully, deliver the load to the waiting ironworkers.

As the skyscraper goes up, there's still work to be done on the ground. The **backhoe** is busy hauling away construction trash.

Foreman's Fact:
A backhoe can do it all—lift, load, and clear with its bucket loader in front, and excavate with its digger in back.

This **forklift** might be small, but it's doing the work of a dozen people. Right now it's bringing a thousand pounds of bricks—in one trip—over to the site elevator.

An **asphalt paver** is laying down hot blacktop for a driveway and a plaza.

And to smooth the asphalt, a compact shovel with a giant wheel is right behind it.

The crew and their trucks have been working hard for months. After working so hard for so long, any crew can grow tired and forgetful. And machines can start to break down. That's when accidents happen.

The crew has to come up with rules to try to prevent accidents.

Some rules are easy, like never walking under a truck's bucket.

But most require teamwork. The crew has to set up barricades around the site. They have to remember to always talk to each other. And they have to double- and *triple*-check their equipment.

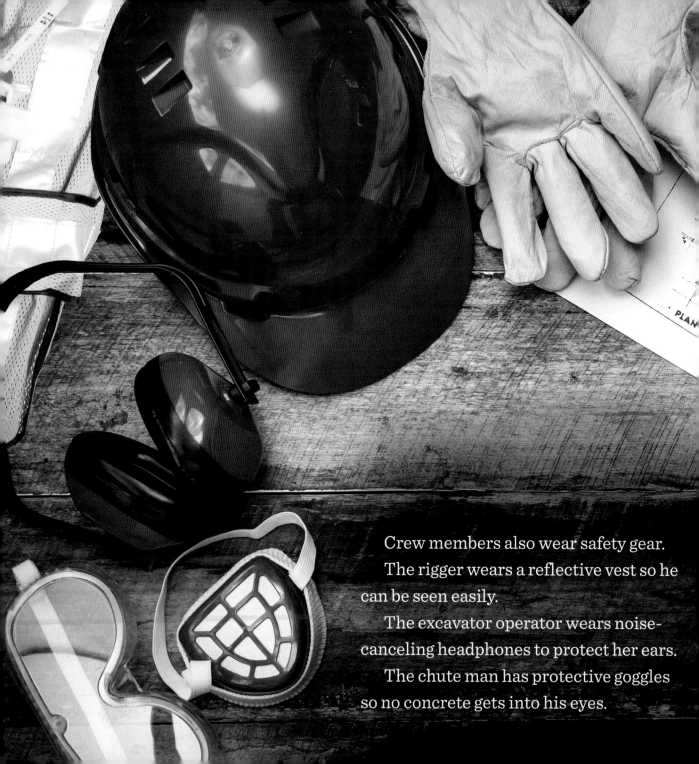

Crew members also wear safety gear. The rigger wears a reflective vest so he can be seen easily.

The excavator operator wears noise-canceling headphones to protect her ears.

The chute man has protective goggles so no concrete gets into his eyes.

Foreman's Fact:
Every single work truck, from a 1,400-ton excavator to a lowly cargo van, makes a steady beeping sound when going in reverse, so no one gets run over.

Even the foreman wears steel-toed boots.

And, of course, everyone is wearing a hard hat.

But working at a construction site won't ever be 100 percent safe. Working with heavy equipment is a serious responsibility and a seriously tough job.

Heavy construction is complete! Now it's up to designers, electricians, plumbers, and other tradespeople to make the inside cozy.

At the end of each day, the trucks are brought to the center of the site, where they're hosed off and refueled. But tomorrow, these trucks won't be needed.

Do you want to start building something new?

Then it's time to head out to find another hard hat zone!